Woodwork
Step-by-Step

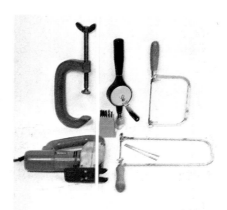

Woodwork
Step-by-Step

Collier Books
A Division of Macmillan Publishing Co., Inc.
New York

A Studio Vista book published by
Cassell & Collier Macmillan Publishers Ltd.,
35 Red Lion Square, London WC1R 4SG,
and at Sydney, Auckland, Toronto, Johannesburg,
an affiliate of Macmillan, Inc., New York

Copyright © Studio Vista, a division
of Cassell and Collier Macmillan Publishers
Ltd., 1976
First published in the U.K. by Studio Vista,
a division of Cassell and Collier Macmillan
Publishers Ltd.
First Collier Books Edition 1976

Macmillan Publishing Co., Inc.
866 Third Avenue, New York, N.Y. 10022

Library of Congress Cataloguing in Publication Data
Main entry under title:
Woodwork.
"A Studio Vista book."
1. Woodwork.
TT185.W658 1976b 684'.08 76-10269
ISBN 0-02-011840-6

Printed in The Netherlands

Contents

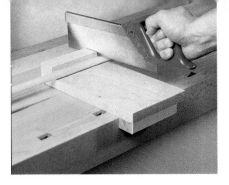

5

1

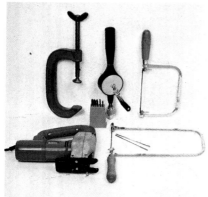

2

3

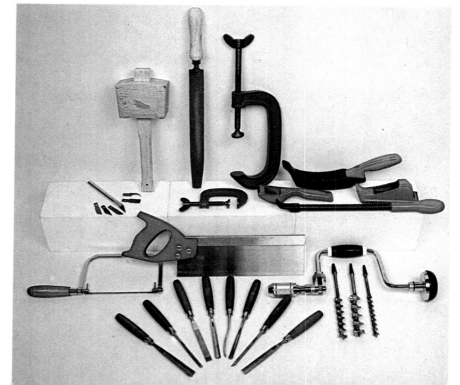

6

Introduction to Woodwork

All the tools and equipment you will need for the woodwork projects in this book are illustrated on this page except for the more specialized tools for veneering (24), picture framing (40) and turning (56). Numbers in brackets refer to pages where a piece of equipment is described in detail.

1 Joinery: from left to right (top row): *jointer plane* (50). (Second row) *Claw hammer. Warrington or tack hammer* for nailing small nails and panel pins or brads. *Bull-nose plane. Smooth plane. Block plane.* (Bottom row) *Adjustable try square. Screwdriver. Spiral screwdriver with ratchet. Marking gauge. Rip saw. Cross cut hand saw. Dovetail or bead saw* – used to cut small mouldings or beads. *Brace* with *auger drill bits. Set of bevel edge chisels* – 6, 12, 19 and 38 mm ($\frac{1}{4}$, $\frac{1}{2}$, $\frac{3}{4}$ and $1\frac{1}{2}$ in.). *Mallet.*

2 Contour cutting: from left to right (top row): *G-cramp (C-clamp). Hand drill* with *twist drill bits* – a set ranging from 1-6 mm (1/16-$\frac{1}{4}$ in.) is not expensive. *Coping saw.* (Bottom row) *Power jig saw (sabre saw). Fret-saw* with *blades* – a medium blade will do for most work.

3 Carving: from left to right (top row): *replaceable blade knife* (20). *Mallet* – buy either the round, carver's mallet or use the ordinary, square carpenter's mallet. *Rasp. G-cramps (C-clamps)* – 15 cm (6 in.) are most versatile. Selection of Surforms. (Bottom row) *Coping saw. Back or tenon saw.* Set of *carving tools* (10). *Brace* with *auger drill bits* – to begin with buy 6 mm, 12 mm and 19 mm ($\frac{1}{4}$, $\frac{1}{2}$ and $\frac{3}{4}$ in.) bits, and buy more as you need them.

Many people today are re-discovering the pleasure of working with their hands and are returning to the traditional craft of woodworking. Almost everyone is familiar with the basic tools of the craft even if they have only used a hammer to hang up a picture. This book is designed to teach you a wide variety of woodworking skills in clear and easy stages. As you work through each project you will gradually build up a basic knowledge of all the woodworking skills from carving to veneering and turning. You don't need a well equipped workshop to make a start. A heavy door or an old, sturdy table set up with a vice in a corner of a room is sufficient to make most of the projects in this book.

There are very few basic rules in woodworking but the most important thing to remember from the beginning is to buy the very best tools you can afford and keep them sharp as you work. In the old-fashioned joinery shops where most work was done by hand, tools were sharpened after each job and carefully replaced in their proper position for the next time. You should form the same habits and stick to them faithfully. That way the tools will always be where you expect them to be and always sharp and ready for use. Refer to pages 62-63 for instructions on sharpening tools and practise putting an edge on your chisels, gouges and plane irons before you use them. This is particularly important in carving.

No one learns woodworking by merely reading about it. Wood is a fascinating material which unlike metal or plastic, varies considerably from species to species and even from tree to tree. The best thing about working with wood is that even as a beginner, you get immediate and satisfying results and the more you learn the more interested you become.

Carving and turning tools courtesy of Record Ridgeway Tools Ltd; all other tools courtesy of Stanley Tools Ltd. Workbench courtesy of Lervad (UK) Ltd.

1 **Pine** (softwood): there are many varieties of pine universally used for building and some furniture.

2 **Mahogany** (hw): Honduras and African are available and widely used for furniture, usually as veneer.

3 **Elm** (hw): good general hardwood for boat building, construction work and turning.

4 **Cedar** (sw): turns grey with age. It is light and strong and used for ladders and window frames.

5 **Douglas fir** (sw): extremely tall trees used in construction work, for plywood and in furniture.

6 **Beech** (hardwood): nice close-grained wood suitable for furniture, turning, toys but not outdoor use.

7 **Oak** (hw): extremely strong and durable for structural work and use in furniture.

8 **Sycamore** (hw): white coloured wood used for furniture and small detail work, e.g. turning.

9 **Teak** (hw): teak from the region of Burma is heavy and durable. Used for furniture and ship work.

10 **Birch** (hw): fairly hard wood, suitable for furniture and general woodworking purposes.

WOOD SAMPLES AND CHARACTERISTICS

The structure of wood

Wood is made up of long and thin cells like drinking straws which carry sap from the roots up to the leaves where it combines with other materials to keep the tree growing. Each species has its own particular cell characteristics and it is this variation which makes mahogany different from oak.

The wood of all trees is formed in the spring and summer, after a period of hibernation in fall and winter. As the new leaves of a tree appear, new cells grow in a very thin layer just inside the bark.

These tubular cells have thin walls and a large central space to carry up the maximum sap during the burst of growth. This spring wood is weak since the tube walls are thin but the summer wood, which is formed as the growth rate slows, has much heavier cell walls and is therefore much stronger.

Each year's growth repeats the cycle and leaves the familiar annual ring of two slightly different coloured cells of spring and summer wood. Count these rings and you can tell the age of the tree.

Trees respond to a particularly severe storm or a bad drought and this alters the cell structure of the rings and forms an historical record of the weather patterns.

As the tree gets older, the inner core is no longer needed to carry sap and it serves the structural function of holding the tree up. This tougher centre wood is called heart wood whereas the softer and usually lighter outer layers make up the sap wood.

Wood 'grain'

The 'grain' of the wood refers to the texture and colour formed on

11 Brown oak (hw): European oak stained brown by an edible fungus. Very valuable as veneer for furniture.

12 Ebony (hw): extremely hard and expensive wood. Used for detail work such as chess men and piano keys.

13 Larch (sw): a hard softwood used for outdoor work both as furniture and flooring.

14 American walnut (hw): also European or African varieties. Excellent for furniture and turning.

15 Ash (hw): very tough and hard. Used for tool handles, baseball and cricket bats. Excellent for turning.

16 Afromosia (hw): from West Africa, it is used in furniture, sometimes stained to resemble mahogany.

17 Bird's eye maple (hw): part of maple with markings from under-developed shoots, used as veneer.

18 Yellow poplar (hw): a light hardwood used chiefly for packing cases, toys and some furniture.

19 Utile (hw): coarse-textured African hardwood used in general furniture work.

20 Zebrawood (hw): an exotic wood from Africa. Used in decorative furniture usually as veneer.

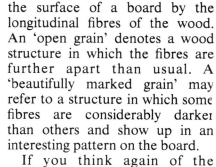

the surface of a board by the longitudinal fibres of the wood. An 'open grain' denotes a wood structure in which the fibres are further apart than usual. A 'beautifully marked grain' may refer to a structure in which some fibres are considerably darker than others and show up in an interesting pattern on the board.

If you think again of the analogy of a bundle of drinking straws you can see why sawing or carving along the fibres is much easier and smoother than cutting across them. Using the same example you can understand why wood splits. Forcing a wedge, chisel or nail between the fibres tends to force them apart and to break the longitudinal bond between them causing a split lengthwise along the grain.

Softwood and hardwood
Softwood and hardwood are slightly misleading terms because, although softwoods are generally softer than hardwoods, there are notable exceptions. Balsa wood which is the softest wood of all is classified as a hardwood.

Softwood comes from the evergreen trees with needle-pointed leaves. It is usually softer and cheaper than hardwood because the trees grow more quickly. Used for building work, joists and some furniture, it is also the source of wood pulp for paper.

The wood from broad-leaved, deciduous trees is classified as hardwood. Since hardwood is usually harder and denser, it is stronger and more durable than softwood and is therefore more valued for woodworking.

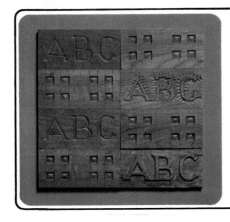

Carving Sampler

You will need:

Several hardwood blocks approx.
150×75 mm (6 × 3 in.), 12 mm
($\frac{1}{2}$ in.) thick
1 piece plywood approx.
300×200 mm (12×8 in.),
12-19 mm ($\frac{1}{2}$-$\frac{3}{4}$ in.) thick
Wood strip 25×12 mm
(1×$\frac{1}{2}$ in.) 200 mm (8 in.) long
7 19-mm ($\frac{3}{4}$-in.) wood screws
Chisels and gouges
V or parting tool
Wooden mallet
G-cramp (C-clamp)

Just like the traditional embroidery samplers these carving samplers will introduce you to the various tools and the basic techniques of the craft.

Instead of practising on a large and expensive piece of wood where you may feel inhibited, use small blocks of wood which will allow you to feel more relaxed about learning to carve. Use any hardwood available, such as teak, mahogany, oak, elm or walnut. If necessary use some of each kind to create a contrasting effect.

Because the fibres of hardwood are packed more tightly together, the wood is 'close-grained' and is therefore easier to sand and polish to a smooth finish. This finer texture also means that the fibres have less tendency to tear and split as you work them.

Buying wood

Most hardwood is now so expensive that you must plan work carefully. All the wood you buy must have been properly dried to a specific moisture content before it is sold. Even after the correct drying a piece of wood will tend to bend and warp as its moisture content changes in a new environment.

To minimize this, select good,

1 Clamp the base to a bench or sturdy table. Hold the block in place with a cam.

2 Use the mallet on the straight chisel to mark the ends of the grooves. Tap lightly to avoid splitting.

3 With hand force only, make several cuts with the gouge. The final cut should leave a smooth surface.

4 This pattern uses a smaller gouge. Make circles by turning gouge around and scooping out centre.

5 Notice the different effect of carving in opposite directions for the two rows.

6 This time the grooves should end gradually. Carve in both directions from the ends.

straight, dry planks and, if possible, leave the wood in a dry place for a month or two before working with it. This way all cracking and warping will take place before and not after you work on the wood.

Avoid all large knots, splits, or any discolouration especially in costly hardwoods.

Try to find a friendly wood dealer who will let you select the wood you want yourself. You not only save money by choosing boards which are precisely the right length, but you also get the chance to find the pieces with the most interesting markings.

Tools

Carving tools come in a variety of shapes and sizes. With a basic set of about eight tools (see page 6), you will be able to do a wide range of carving cuts.

Gouges are U-shaped in section but vary in both width and curvature. So a 12 mm ($\frac{1}{2}$ in.) wide gouge comes in shapes which vary from the nearly flat to the sharply curved.

Chisels are perfectly flat, but the cutting edge may be square across like ordinary chisels or angled.

Any basic tool kit will include

several gouges of various widths and curves, one straight and one screw chisel and one V-tool or parting tool which is used to make fine cuts and grooves. You will also need a wooden mallet: either the ordinary beech carpenter's mallet or the special round wood carver's mallet.

Holding the work

There are various ways of holding the work steady against a work-bench or table. For flat pieces you can clamp a plywood base to the bench. Use two wood screws to attach short strips of wood on

7 The mistake where the gouge slipped does not ruin the block. Don't discard mistakes like this.

8 Mark out squares to the size of the chisel then cut 3 mm ($\frac{1}{8}$ in.) deep cuts on four sides.

9 Start at centre and gradually slice deeper toward the edge cut using the same straight chisel.

10 Repeat this cut in the other three directions leaving a pyramid shape in the centre.

11 Arrange the six leaves in a circle. Use the mallet to cut along circle and outer curved edges.

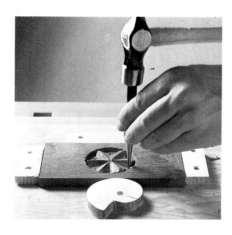

12 Either cut a cross on large nail head or use nail punch to make texture on background.

three sides of the block (**1**). For the fourth side make a small plywood cam (see **1**) which can be finger-tightened against the block and released quickly.

The cam is simple to make. Cut out a circular piece of plywood with a coping saw (see pages 33-35) and screw it off-centred to the base. Or make the cam shown here by gradually increasing the radius of the circle from 12 mm ($\frac{1}{2}$ in.) to about 40 mm ($1\frac{1}{2}$ in.).

Using the tools

To get the feel of the tools you should try cutting in various directions, with both the left and right hand if possible. Most cuts can be made using only the force of your hands to guide the gouge through the wood, but where more pressure is required, you must use the mallet.

Study the photographs for each sampler and draw the pattern lightly on the block with a pencil and ruler. The channels should of course be the same width as the gouges you intend to use.

Notice that when cutting along the grain, the gouge will tend to slip in one direction and bite into the wood and tear off chunks in the opposite direction.

In the first two samplers (**1-6**), practise cutting in each direction and also across the grain, i.e. perpendicular to the grain, and learn to control the gouge. Everyone makes mistakes at first so don't be put off; it is the only way to learn.

For the next sampler (**7-9**) use the straight chisel to chip carve this familiar indented pyramid design. This pattern can be used to decorate the edges of furniture or shelves.

The last few blocks use the same basic techniques to make more complicated patterns. To make the floral pattern (**10-12**) use a gouge to outline the shapes and

then the straight or skew chisel to carve out the leaf detail.

An entirely different and interesting carving effect is incised lettering. The letters are first carefully drawn or preferably traced through carbon paper. You can achieve the opposite effect by carving away the background to set out the letters (**16**) or pattern (**17**) in relief.

Try to make at least two blocks of each pattern to get enough practice. Remember that you should never sand a relief wood carving. Work in even strokes. Be sure to keep the tools sharp with constant sharpening so that the carved edges will be smooth and even. Sharp tools will make a tremendous difference in the finished result (see pages 62-63).

Displaying the blocks

Use your imagination in arranging the blocks. They will look delightful just glued to a piece of background plywood and hung on the wall. Another useful idea for displaying the samplers is to arrange them around a mirror or picture frame. Glue or screw the blocks to a plywood backing to hold them together.

13 Make a cut approximately 3 mm ($\frac{1}{8}$ in.) deep along centre lines. Use a narrow gouge for tight curves.

14 After scoring outline with knife make careful cuts with chisels or gouge toward centre.

15 Create letters in relief by first cutting along outline and then removing the background.

16 The same relief effect with oak leaves. Notice the grooved background made with a gouge.

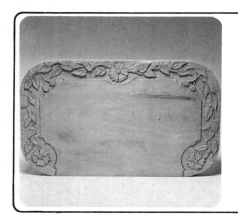

Breadboard

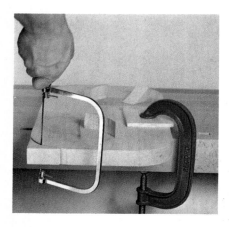

1 Use a clean, knot-free piece of hardwood. Mark and cut a radius at each corner.

2 Smooth the corners with a Surform. Use the lines as a guide and sand smooth.

You will need:
1 piece hardwood (beech or
    similar) approx 400×250 mm
    (16×10 in.), 20-30 mm
    ($\frac{3}{4}$-$1\frac{1}{4}$ in.) thick
Carving tools
Coping saw
Surform
G-cramp (C-clamp)

Carving the sampler with the oak leaves should have given you some practice in relief carving. There are many applications for this type of carving and one of the simplest is to make a breadboard.

You can make the design as complicated or as simple as you like. You could spell out the letters 'bread' around the edge of the board or use a fruit and leaf motif like this one. In this example, the cherry leaves and fruit and flowers are used as a repeating motif.

Carving the leaves
After the background has been removed the leaves look rather shapeless. The final effect of relief carving depends on creating a variety of realistic shapes. Study the appearance of real leaves on a branch and then copy the curling and rounded shapes in your car-

ving. It also helps to remove the wood from under the edges of the carving to allow the leaves to stand out more.

Everyone makes mistakes on a carving of this size and you may find that it is difficult to keep pieces of leaves and blossoms from breaking off as you carve. There is no way of preventing this except to be careful, take your time and keep the tools very sharp. The carving can usually be 'doctored' by removing a little more background and reshaping the leaves and flowers.

If your tool is dull you may try to over-compensate by pushing the gouge harder. That is usually when the delicate pieces break off. So remember to use the oil stone and leather strop frequently to keep your tools sharp (see pages 62-3).

Relief carving
Relief carving is extremely versatile and quite simple compared with the more complicated three-dimensional carving. Carving designs range from simple motifs such as oak or maple leaves to much more complex designs.

Now that you know the problems of creating a carving in

3 Transfer design by taping half drawing to board over carbon paper. Repeat on other side of centre line.

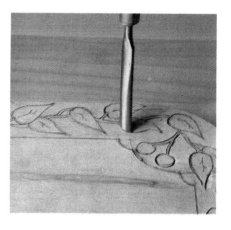

4 Start by cutting vertically along outline. Be careful not to remove the thin branches.

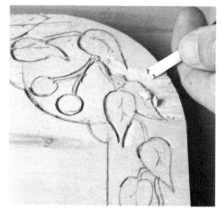

5 After removing background with a deep gouge, try to cut under the leaves to make them stand out.

6 Use your judgement in shaping the leaves. Notice the grooves which are cut with the V or parting tool.

wood you will begin to appreciate carvings on furniture and buildings and, in particular, in churches where the master wood-carver practised his art to the fullest.

Motifs such as fleur-de-lys, chains of overlapping circles and scrolls are quite common, but each craftsman developed his own patterns. Study these motifs and then adapt them to make up your own variations. When you have developed enough confidence you can turn your furniture such as table legs into hand-crafted articles by adding touches of carving.

Bowl

1 Measure the wood, then draw the bowl about 15 mm ($\frac{5}{8}$ in.) thick. Make inside and outside templates.

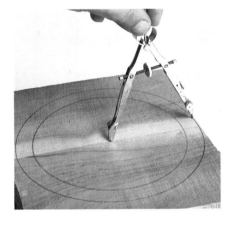

2 Draw the inside and outside circles on the top and the bottom circles on the bottom.

3 Cut away as much as possible with a hand saw in order to save extra work later on.

4 Screw wood to base and drill holes in top within inside circle. Note the homemade depth gauge.

You will need:
1 piece hardwood approx.
    150-200 mm (6-8 in.) square,
    50-75 mm (2-3 in.) thick
Plywood base approx.
    300×200 mm (12×8 in.), 12 or
    19 mm ($\frac{1}{2}$ or $\frac{3}{4}$ in.) thick
3 or 4 25-mm (1-in.) wood screws
Carving tools
Surforms or rasps
Brace and bit
Compass

Any attractive hardwood such as elm, beech, walnut, teak or mahogany is suitable for a carved bowl.

The quickest way to make bowls is of course to turn them on a lathe (see pages 56-9). But hand carved bowls with their irregularities are often more distinguished than the machine made, turned bowls.

Carving the bowl
Because it is more difficult to smooth the bottom of a deep bowl, the beginner should start with a fairly shallow one, say about 50 mm (2 in.) deep. Remove most of the wood inside by drilling holes first; be careful not to drill through the bottom or the sides. To prevent this you can make a

5 Using a large gouge and mallet, cut away wood from the inside. Be careful to stay within circle.

6 Remove bowl from base and round with a Surform. Use two G-cramps (C-clamps) instead of a vice.

7 Check the profile frequently. The point of contact with the template shows where to remove the wood.

8 Screw bowl back on base and finish carving inside. Leave the grooves or smooth it down inside.

9 Use the inside template frequently to check the shape. Small variations in shape are permitted.

10 Complete the bowl by shaping the top edge. Finally, sand the outside smooth.

depth gauge by passing the drill through a piece of wood to leave just enough of the drill bit exposed (**4**).

Finishing the bowl
The inside of the bowl should be well-sanded inside and out. Start with rough sandpaper, then medium and finally finish with fine paper. Before the final sanding, moisten the bowl with a damp rag.

The nicest finish is several coats of wax rubbed into the wood (see pages 60-61) but the finish you choose will depend on the wood you choose and the bowl's use.

Fruit Carving

1 Trace the banana shape on the wood on both sides, looking at the markings on the wood.

You will need:
For bananas: small block of any hardwood at least 40×40 mm (1½×1½ in.) and approx. 150 mm (6 in.) long
For apples: 60 mm (2¼ in.) any hardwood cubes
Coping saw
Back or hand saw
Sharp whittling or trimming (utility) knife
Surform or rasp

Fruit carving is a very old and popular craft and provides excellent practice in modelling. It only requires bits of hardwood

2 Cut out the shape with a coping saw. Very hard woods heat the blade so stop to allow it to cool.

you may find discarded by sawmills or furniture factories.

Carving the banana
Always use a real-life model and refer to it frequently as you go along. Remove a bit of wood and then check the carving against the real banana.

The tip of the banana tends to break off as you are carving, so the instructions include an easy method of glueing another back.

Carving the apple
The shape of the apple is a little easier to carve than the banana

3 Nail back one of the cut off sides and use it as a guide for the other identical profile.

although it lends itself to more detailed carving. The stem on the top and the little rosette on the bottom are a challenge to carve.

Finishing
You may have noticed how beautifully finished fruit carvings are. There are several ways of achieving a glass-like finish but for any of the methods (see page 60) you must first sandpaper very thoroughly, moistening the wood before the final sanding. Then you can either simply apply several coats of wax polish, or a varnish sealer followed by polish.

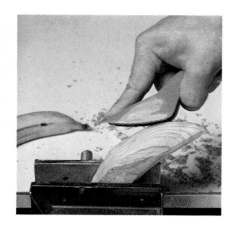

4 Holding it in a vice, shape the banana with a Surform or rasp, referring to the real banana.

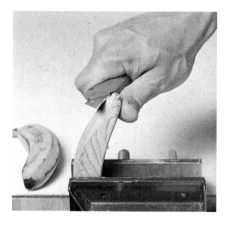

5 Whittle the ends with a sharp knife. Hold the wood in your hand if that is easier.

6 If the long end breaks off, put another on by glueing in a piece of matchstick in both sides.

7 Trace the apple in the same way. Try to use wood with a pronounced and interesting grain pattern.

8 Carefully copy the end details. A sturdy knife with replaceable blades is very useful.

Duck Carving

1 Study the shape, then draw the front and top views and trace onto wood with carbon paper.

2 Use a coping saw to cut along the lines. Don't worry if the sawing looks uneven at this stage.

You will need:
Body: 1 piece softwood
  50×45 mm (2×1¾ in), 200 mm (8 in.) long
Head: 1 piece softwood
  50×15 mm (2×⅝ in.), 75 mm (3 in.) long
1 black or brown map pin for eye
Coping saw
Surform
Sharp whittling knife
Sandpaper
Glue

Bird carving is extremely popular, particularly in North America where duck decoy carving has been practised for centuries.

The most popular wood for bird carving is bass wood or linden but it may be difficult to find. In the early stages, ordinary pine is a good substitute, but remember to select good, dry samples which are free from pitch, knots and other faults. If cracks or splits develop as you carve, you can fill them with any commercial wood filler. Once sanded over, the crack will be left smooth and it will not show at all after you paint the decoy.

After the initial shaping of the body with Surforms, draw knives or other tools, you will have to carve the detail with a very

sharp knife. There are several replaceable-blade knives on the market. Select a robust knife which has several blade shapes.

Before starting on the bird, try a few whittling strokes on a piece of waste wood. Notice the way the knife sometimes digs into the grain and tends to tear away large chunks. After a little practice you will get a feeling for the wood and be able to prevent this.

There are several ways of using the knife. You can whittle toward the body, actually towards the thumb (**6**). This method is quite easy and natural and it affords good control for detailed work.

Another method is to hold the knife in the right hand but push the blade from behind with the left thumb. This way also offers good control. Find the method which is most comfortable and natural for you.

Painting the decoy
Oil paints are the easiest to use and produce the most lifelike effect. The photographs of the finished ducks show how simply antique decoys were painted. They have a certain charm that modern realistically painted decoys lack.

3 Don't throw away the piece with the drawing. Nail it back and cut off the other sides.

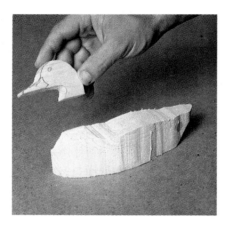

4 After cutting out the head, glue it to the body. Hold the pieces together with a couple of skew nails.

5 Shape the body to look natural. It should be widest in the centre and taper toward the back and front.

6 Carefully shape the head which should be thin at the top and throat and puffy in the cheeks.

7 Sand with rough paper. Note the flat tapering shape of the bill. It is about 6 mm ($\frac{1}{4}$ in.) wide.

8 Copy the wing detail as shown. Note the shape of the tail feathers and knot which will be filled later.

9 Continue whittling away wood on the back side, so the primaries come to a point under the tertials.

photograph by Chris Overton

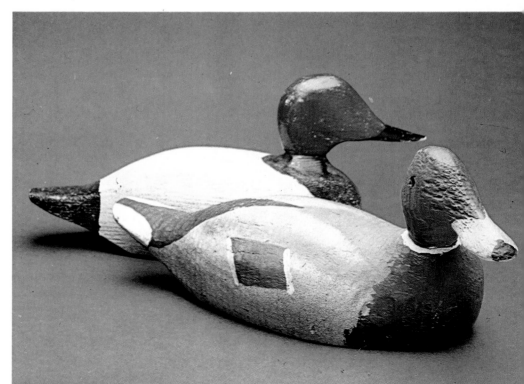

Veneer Carving

1 Thoroughly cover the surface with a thin layer of glue. Use a small brush to smooth down.

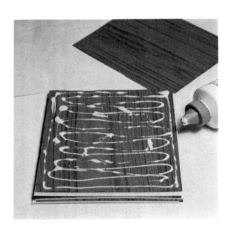

2 Clamp about 20 layers of veneer between pieces of sturdy plywood. Glue three chunks into one piece.

You will need:
A total of 50-60 pieces veneer
    approx. 200 mm (8 in.) square,
    25-30 pieces light veneer
    (sycamore) and 25-30 dark
    veneer (mahogany or teak)
Carving tools
Coping saw
Surforms
G-cramp (C-clamp)
Glue, preferably animal

Most craftsmen prefer to think up their own designs to make their work unique. Their inspiration usually comes from keeping their eyes alert for strange and interesting shapes that can be adapted for wood sculpture.

Nature is a good source of inspiration. Walking through a park or forest one can find hundreds of ideas in natural forms. The shapes of leaves or branches for example would lend themselves well to wood sculpture. It is an interesting project to start with a found branch and to carve it following its natural patterns. You may well find that you do not have to do very much to it before an exciting shape emerges. After adding a subtle finish (see page 60) you will have an object you will be pleased to display.

Another good source of design ideas is the seashore. Shells and weathered logs and even the sand dunes are gracefully shaped, and can all inspire the craftsman.

In this example, a simple scallop shell is carved out of a piece of wood made by glueing together alternate layers of light and dark veneers.

Veneers are actually very thin pieces of wood peeled off the log when it is wet. They are used mostly as a thin decorative layer for furniture but they are also interesting to experiment with for other uses (see pages 24-32).

If veneers aren't available, you can improvise by glueing together thicker pieces of wood in various colour patterns. Any woodworking glue can be used, but remember to clamp the layers together well and allow the glue to dry thoroughly before carving.

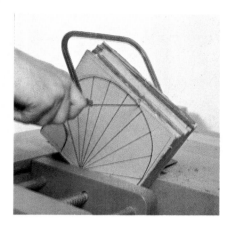

3 Draw the design on both sides copying the shell. Then cut out the shape with the coping saw.

4 Screw the shell flat to plywood which is clamped to bench. Carefully gouge out inside. Note the ridges.

5 Shape the back with a Surform. Refer often to the actual shell to get a realistic shape.

Veneered Table

1 Steel ruler, iron, coping saw, veneering hammer, veneering saw, craft knives.

2 Before veneering the top, follow these instructions for veneering the underside with 'inferior' veneer.

3 Complete the underside and nail on edging. Make it flush with the top so top veneer covers edge.

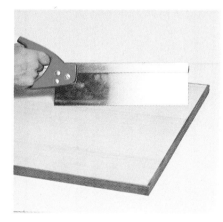

4 Scrape the surface by drawing the back saw (or other saw) across it. This provides a key for the glue.

You will need:
1 piece plywood approx. 750×500 mm (30×20 in), 19 mm ($\frac{3}{4}$ in.) thick
High grade veneer (mahogany or similar) to cover surface 750×500 mm (30×20 in.)
Inferior grade veneer to cover underside, same size as high grade
Mahogany stripping or edging 19 mm ($\frac{3}{4}$ in.) wide, approx. 2.7 m (9 ft) long to cover edge
4 table legs with screws
Back saw
Veneering saw (optional)
Veneering hammer
Hammer
Trimming (utility) knife
Steel ruler
Iron
Scotch, pearl or hot hide glue
Glue pot
Sponge or rag

Veneer
As some woods like rosewood or walnut get scarcer and more expensive, less and less of it is sold in ordinary solid boards. Instead, the wood is sliced up using very sophisticated machinery into very thin sheets of less than 1 mm ($\frac{1}{32}$ in.) thick. These are then either made into plywood or glued onto

5 Swab the top side of veneer with hot water to prevent it from curling up as it touches the glue.

6 Spread the glue on base and lay veneer. Then press down by zig-zagging veneering hammer toward edges.

7 Lay second sheet and allow glue to set. Cut through overlap with knife using steel edge as guide.

8 Heat to release glue then pull out end. Press down again and hold with masking tape.

9 Turn upside down and trim overlap. A veneer saw is useful for cross-grain cutting but a sharp knife will do.

10 After sanding edges and setting nails, screw in legs according to the instructions on the package.

less expensive wood for use as furniture.

Most veneers are peeled from the log which has been steamed or boiled to soften it.

Today modern synthetic glues have replaced the traditional animal glues used for veneering. But the old-fashioned technique still has many advantages, particularly for the amateur who doesn't have a clamping press.

Select the strips of veneer and lay them down one by one. On plywood they are laid perpendicular to the top plywood layer, on solid wood along the grain.

To prevent the board from warping as the glue dries and pulls the veneer, it is necessary to add a compensating veneer on the underside. Start by veneering the underside. You will then have had some experience before laying the veneer on the top.

First the glue, which is available in cake, flake or powdered form, must be heated (but not boiled) with enough water to make it easy to work with. Heat it in an electric glue pot or, as here, in an improvised double boiler. Score the plywood with a sideways

movement of a saw, and apply a thin layer of glue. The scores in the wood make the surface more receptive to the glue.

Lay the first sheet of veneer (5) and use a veneer hammer to press it down on the plywood surface (6). Move the hammer in a zigzag motion starting in the centre and working towards the edges, to remove any air bubbles trapped under the veneer.

Lay the second sheet overlapping the first after carefully removing the dried glue from the side and surface of the first sheet with a scraper.

Veneer Lamp

1 Cut 12 veneer pieces about 15cm (6 in.) wide. Make six 75 cm (30 in.) long and six 63 cm (25 in.) long.

You will need:
12 strips light veneer approx.
   150 mm (6 in.) wide, 6 strips
   750 mm (30 in.) long, 6 strips
   630 mm (25 in.) long
2 pieces plywood 150×150 mm
   (6×6 in.), 6 mm ($\frac{1}{4}$ in.) thick
Electric wire and bulb holder
Coping saw
Hand drill
Trimming (utility) knife
Steel ruler
Contact adhesive

Veneer can be used for many things besides furniture surfaces. In Scandinavia designers have

imaginatively used veneer for a variety of lampshades.

Remember, during the assembly of a lamp to spread the glue on both surfaces and allow the contact adhesive to become touch dry before pressing the surfaces together hard. It is better to be patient than to find that the glue comes undone when the lamp is nearly finished. If you find the veneer very springy and hard to secure, put a few staples or tacks through each veneer after glueing.

Use the veneer leftovers to experiment with other shapes like cylindrical or Tiffany lamps.

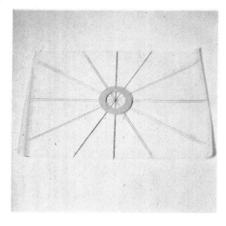

2 Cut two 15 cm (6 in.) diameter plywood discs, one with 9 cm (3½ in.) hole. Lay on pattern.

3 First glue down six short strips in opposite pairs. Align them symmetrically around lines in pattern.

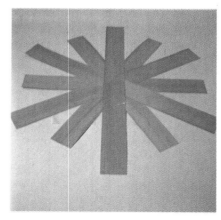

4 Now glue down six long strips the same way. Secure with staples or small tacks at intervals.

5 Turn over and cut through veneers inside the disc area. Smooth edges by sanding.

6 Glue the leaves in opposite pairs starting with the top one. Top disc has 12 mm ($\frac{1}{2}$ in.) hole.

7 The last leaves are awkward so put arm through bottom and hold to press from underneath.

8 Drill or cut a hole through the veneers. Start working from inside the lamp.

9 Pass a wire through the small hole and connect the bulb holder. The shade hangs from the holder.

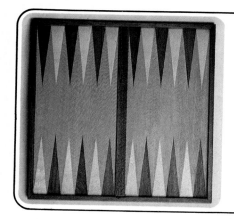

Game Boards

1   Hold rule against spacing guides.
Cut 5 strips of each colour 45 mm
(1$\frac{3}{4}$ in.) wide and 38 cm (15 in.) long.

2   Leave the cutting guides and,
after taping together alternate strips,
cut chequered strips.

3   Tape these strips together and
trim to eight squares. Four extra strips
are for the border.

4   After allowing glue to become
touch-dry, carefully lay the sheet
starting at one edge.

Today almost all veneering is done
using modern resin glues. These
have an advantage over the
traditional animal glues because
they form a more permanent
bond, cause less shrinkage, and
also allow very little penetration of
glue through the veneer. For
smaller pieces you can arrange a
homemade press similar to that
used for the shell (see page 22).

The impact adhesive used for
this gameboard is not really

5 Either use a mallet or your fist to make sure surfaces are thoroughly joined.

6 Nail and glue edging to plywood edge. You don't have to mitre corners but if you want to, see page 41.

7 Tape together band for surround. Make the sides overlap at corners and cut at 45° away from corner.

suitable for professional veneering jobs. But since it requires no continuous pressure it is often used for small projects. You must arrange the veneers carefully because once contact is made between the glued surfaces you can't slide the veneer into position.

Splicing Veneers

With animal glues you can cut and re-position the veneers after the glue has been applied, but for resin or impact adhesives the veneers must be matched, cut, and taped together into one reasonably accurately matched piece before glueing.

A quick and accurate method of measuring off the veneer strips is to use a cutting board. You can make this cutting board (**1** and **2**) by screwing a straight piece of stripping along the edge of a piece of plywood approximately 60×20 cm (24×8 in.). Cut 75 mm (3 in.) long slots at either end to fit a 6 mm ($\frac{1}{4}$ in.) bolt and wing nut. Pass these through a short length of dowel and then locate the bolts so that they serve as a guide to the steel ruler.

The most important thing to remember is to cut through the

veneer in several strokes. For the first cut you should only score the veneer lightly. Remember this technique in cutting any sheet material with a knife.

Once you have taped the veneer strips together cutting across the alternate bands (**2**) can present difficulties. The light strips are usually softer, and the knife tends to get caught in the dark strips and tear them. If this happens try to tape the pieces back together and cut very gently across them.

BACKGAMMON BOARD

A backgammon board is also quite easy to make. The only new technique to be learnt involves matching the sharp V-shapes.

Draw the zigzag configuration on the main veneer and carefully tape small rectangular strips of the two other shades to the underside.

Then cut along the marks through both layers, remove the waste, and tape the veneers together. The fit will be nearly perfect.

Finally glue down the two sides of the board and cover the centre strip with a piece of the same material used for the edges.

8 After trimming edge of veneer and setting panel pins (brads), sand along the grain with garnet paper.

29

Jewelry Box

1 You need a choice of veneers, box and drawing. You may prefer to cover only the top in marquetry.

You will need:
Several shades of veneer
Sheets of light 'waste' veneer
    e.g. sycamore
Wooden box
Trimming knife (utility)
Steel ruler
Impact adhesive
Masking tape

Marquetry is a type of veneering in which small pieces of veneer are joined to make a picture or pattern. There are various methods of marquetry each with its particular advantages but the 'Window' method that is shown

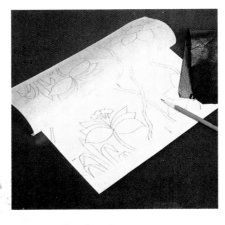

2 Tape the drawing to waste veneer and transfer drawing through carbon paper. Note the guide marks.

here is probably the easiest to follow.

Basically, the procedure is to transfer a drawing to a piece of light waste veneer and then, by cutting out sections or windows, replace the waste veneer with the pieces of the final veneer which go to make up the design.

Although marquetry requires patience and careful attention to each detail, it's really not difficult. There are marquetry societies all over the world which indicates what an absorbing and international hobby it has become.

One of the advantages of the

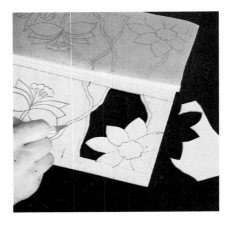

3 Cut out the largest piece. Remember first to score and then cut through veneer with light strokes.

window method is that it allows you to pass the opening over the veneer to select the best section of it before cutting. Marquetry enthusiasts spend a lot of time searching for interesting veneers which are cut from sections of the tree where the grain twists and curls. These veneers are especially valued. Curl veneers for example are cut near the intersection of a branch and the trunk of the tree, whereas burr veneers come from the wartlike growths which occur on some trees.

The jewelry box
For the first try, it might be wise to

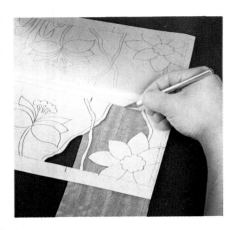

4 Move 'window' over chosen veneer to find the nicest area. Score veneer, remove and cut out shape.

5 Place piece in window and tape in place. Normally only one window would be cut at a time.

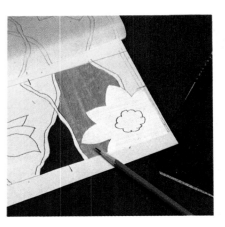

6 Once the flower piece is added the centre drawing is lost. Re-draw with tracing and carbon paper.

7 All the pieces in place. The area is slightly larger than the box top to allow for trimming.

do just the top of the box and cover the sides in single pieces of veneer. You can use any box with a removable or hinged top or you can make one yourself out of hardwood (see pages 46-47). Before applying the marquetry, remove any old finish by sanding thoroughly. This flower motif wraps around all the sides and top and requires careful attention so that the figures line up from one surface to another. You can do any design you like in marquetry, perhaps a rectangular geometric pattern, although nature scenes seem to be the most popular ones.

Of course you can cheat a little and buy a marquetry kit which contains stencils for the design and all the veneers you will need for the finished piece.

Remember, never cut through the veneer in one stroke, because the knife will tend to follow the grain and the wood will split along and not across the grain.

When you have finished piecing together the veneers, don't worry about the gaps between the pieces. These are bound to occur and you can easily cheat a little and fill them adding a sprinkling of wood dust to clear glue.

After glueing down the finished piece (see page 28-29), you can either scrape the surface lightly and carefully with a scraper or use fine sandpaper or garnet paper to get a smooth surface prior to finishing.

The best finish is the least complicated one – a simple wax finish of either straight beeswax or a mixture of three or four parts beeswax to one part carnauba wax if available (see pages 60-61).

8 Now apply glue (see pages 28-29). Glue to base surface. Tap it well to guarantee good contact.

9 Trim edges carefully with knife. It is very important not to tear the delicate pieces. Score several times.

Contour Cutting

1 Cut the 4 mm (⅛ in.) plywood in pieces for each animal. Trace animal shapes.

2 Transfer the tracing to the wood by scribbling on the back along the line then retracing from the front.

You will need:
1 piece plywood 600×600 mm
   (24×24 in,), 4 mm (⅛ in.) thick
   5 12 mm (½ in.) diameter dowels,
    900 mm (36 in.) long
Back saw or handsaw
Coping saw
Hand drill
Paint
String or thread

Contour cutting

This is perhaps the simplest technique in woodworking and it is remarkably useful. With only one or two inexpensive tools the beginner can make a wide variety of delightful projects, particularly children's toys and puzzles. And it doesn't require a work bench; a piece of plywood clamped to a table (**8**) is all you need to do jig saw work.

Most people refer to nearly all saws which cut contours as jig saws, but in fact, only the electric table model is correctly called a jig saw.

The coping saw (see **2**, page 6) and the fret-saw are the two hand-held jig saws most frequently used. The coping saw has an adjustable handle which is loosened to fit the blade and also to rotate the direction of the blade.

The fret-saw (see pages 36-37) has more distance between the blade and the body and can therefore reach further in from the edge of the work. It is used more for fine hobby work like cutting veneers for marquetry, for scrollworks, and for making jigsaw puzzles.

There are also power jig saws. The portable, hand-held types (also called sabre saws) are unsuitable for very fine work because the blades are not fine enough to turn and saw tight curves. The bench or table jig saw which is mounted on a stand is perfect for all hobby work but tends to be fairly expensive.

Unless you plan to do a lot of jig saw work, the less expensive hand-held types are perfectly satisfactory.

Using a coping saw

A coping saw is most frequently used vertically in an up and down motion, but it can of course be used any way that is convenient. The blade is added by loosening the handle and fitting the top of the blade first with the teeth pointing toward the handle. Then the handle is tightened until the blade is quite taut.

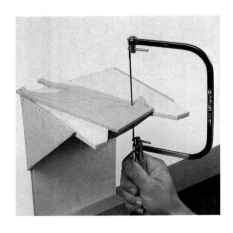

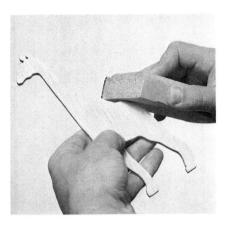

3 Saw along the line with long, even strokes. Hold the work firmly and rotate it with the left hand.

4 Cut out each animal and sand the edges until smooth. Then stain or paint the plywood shapes.

5 Make feet by glueing two strips of wood to the base. Use small clamps or vice until glue sets.

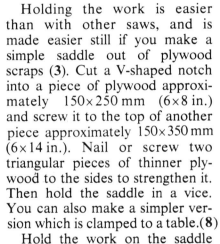

Holding the work is easier than with other saws, and is made easier still if you make a simple saddle out of plywood scraps (**3**). Cut a V-shaped notch into a piece of plywood approximately 150×250 mm (6×8 in.) and screw it to the top of another piece approximately 150×350 mm (6×14 in.). Nail or screw two triangular pieces of thinner plywood to the sides to strengthen it. Then hold the saddle in a vice. You can also make a simpler version which is clamped to a table.(**8**)

Hold the work on the saddle and saw using the longest stroke possible to avoid overheating the blade. Using smooth, even strokes the blade will cut through thin material like 6 or 3 mm ($\frac{1}{4}$ or $\frac{1}{8}$ in.) plywood quite easily. With thicker or harder wood the cutting goes much more slowly and it is advisable to stop and let the blade cool at intervals.

When you cut a curve, move the work around rather than moving the saw. In some cases you will need to change the angle of the blade by adjusting the handle and the top knob.

Notice that the saw mark is quite neat along the top but that underneath the wood fibres are

6 Cut out the handle shape and drill a hole in the handle space. Repeat for the long bottom slot.

7 Release the top of the blade and thread it through the hole. Then re-tighten the blade.

8 Cut the opening for the handle. Note the simple holding device which is clamped to table or workbench.

splintered along the cut. When it is important that both sides are clean cuts, prevent this by placing a piece of thin waste wood under the work and holding the two tightly together as you saw.

When cutting holes in wood you must, of course, first get the saw blade into the opening. First drill a hole within the opening (**6**) then undo the top fixture of the blade and thread it through the hole. After re-tightening the blade you can cut along the lines as before.

The animal shapes

Trace animal shapes like giraffes, lions, tigers, elephants etc. from books and magazines. Then simply transfer the tracing onto plywood and cut out the shapes. You can use the animals simply as they are by making foot stands (**5**) or in any number of imaginative ways.

In the example shown, the animals were painted in bright basic colours and suspended from dowels, to be used as a hanging in a child's room. The animals can

of course be cut out in any size, even life size, and painted as realistically as you like. It would not be difficult to cut out say a large elephant or camel and make it into a toy for the children to ride.

Making a handbag

These handles can be made out of 6 mm ($\frac{1}{4}$ in.) thick plywood. Remember to cut holes in the handles large enough for comfortable carrying; and smooth all edges well so they do not catch hands or clothes.

Jigsaw Puzzle

1 Spread a thin, even layer of rubber adhesive on the board and back of the picture.

2 After the glue is touch-dry, bring the surfaces together carefully starting at one edge.

You will need:
1 piece plywood 4 mm ($\frac{1}{8}$ in.) thick
Drawing or picture
Fret-saw
Rubber-based adhesive

Most children love jigsaw puzzles and you can make the puzzles much more personal by making them yourself. They are very easy to make and cost no more than the small pieces of plywood used for the base. All you have to do is to glue any picture you like onto the plywood and then cut it into various, interlocking shapes.

The picture
You can make puzzles out of any picture you choose: an interesting photograph from a magazine, a drawing, or even a cartoon strip. It is even more fun to make puzzles using drawings the children have done themselves. Then, when the puzzle has lost its appeal as a toy, it can be glued to a backing cardboard and hung on the wall.

Glueing the picture
It is most important that the picture is carefully glued down so that it doesn't lift off as you are sawing and so that it can withstand a certain amount of wear and tear

3 To remove any air pockets, flatten the surface with your palm, working outwards from the centre.

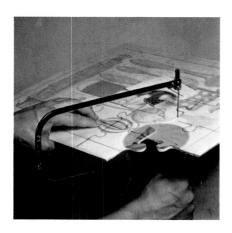

4 Tape a tracing of the piece onto the plywood and cut out using the fret-saw.

later. Use a rubber-based adhesive available in any stationery store, and spread a thin, even coat of the glue on both the plywood and the back of the picture (**1**). Make sure you cover the entire surface, particularly the corners and edges.

Allow the glue to dry for five to 10 minutes until it is touch-dry. Then very carefully bring the glued surfaces together. Start by holding the picture in place over the plywood. Then bring one edge into contact (**2**). Once the surfaces are in contact you won't be able to move them easily so be sure to align them correctly.

After the entire surface is in place smooth it down with the palm of the hand or fist, starting in the centre and working out toward the edges to remove any air pockets. Place a piece of tracing paper over the surface if you think you might smudge the drawing.

The fret-saw
Unlike the coping saw, the blade of the fret-saw cannot be rotated so you must turn the work as the cutting process goes around corners. There are a variety of blades for the fret-saw ranging from fine

to coarse. A medium grade blade is ideal for jigsaw puzzles.

It is important to bear in mind that you can only saw as far in from the edge as the arm of the fret-saw will allow. Therefore you can only use a picture that is less than twice this measurement in both width and length to be able to cut out the middle.

Study other puzzles before setting out the cutting diagram. Each piece must be an interlocking key shape if the jigsaw is to be successful.

1 Draw a tree on one half of the sheet. Notice the straight edges at top and bottom on both sides.

2 Cut out shapes with power jig saw (sabre saw). To make internal cuts, drill hole (see pages 33-35).

Screen

You will need:
2 pieces plywood 1.5×1.22 m (5×4 ft), 10 mm ($\frac{3}{8}$ in.) thick
3 pairs 38 mm ($1\frac{1}{2}$ in.) brass (or steel) hinges with brass machine screws and nuts
Power jig saw (sabre saw)
Hand drill
Screwdriver
G-cramp (C-clamp) (optional)

As you build up your workshop, a power jig saw is an extremely useful tool to buy. Some even have attachments so that you can make perfectly straight cuts or circular cuts with ease. They use a variety of blades depending on the material (wood or metal) and its thickness. Power jig saws are particularly useful for cutting out plywood shapes and it's very easy to guide the saw accurately along any line marked on the wood.

Drawing the trees
In order to fit two trees on one sheet of plywood, first draw a line exactly down the middle of the sheet. Then draw the tree on one side (**1**) making sure that it has a short length of straight side both near the top and at the bottom. This will butt up against the next tree with the hinges screwed in

place.

When cutting the tree put the plywood sheet on sawhorses, trestles or spanning over the backs of two chairs so that the blade doesn't cut into anything underneath and be careful with the saw.

Adding hinges
Attaching the hinges is quite easy, but again requires careful attention. Lay out the trees side by side on the floor or bench. Hold their bases against a straight edge (**4**) and make sure that the flat sections touch, both at the base and at the top.

Decorating the screen
A kitchen or living room scheme may call for more detailed decoration, but if the screen is intended for the children's room, a more whimsical decoration can be used.

You can cut out veneer apples with a coping saw or a fret-saw (see pages 24-32) and then spray paint on the apples in bright colours and glue them to the trees.

There are endless things to make using this convenient saw such as dog kennels, racing cars, circular table tops, play houses and so on.

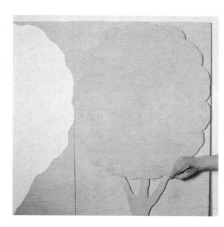

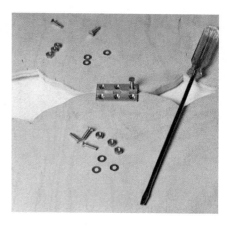

3 Use this tree to trace the three other trees. Make sure to align it exactly so they are all the same.

4 Use hinge to mark holes. Then drill straight through. Use drill bit the same size as the screw.

5 Attach hinge by tightening screws and nuts. Use machine screws as this plywood is too thin for wood screws.

Picture Framing

1 Left: mitre box, panel saw, steel ruler. Right: hammer, frame clamp, craft knife, nail punch.

2 A selection of frames which you stain, paint or leave natural to suit the subject to be framed.

You will need:

Moulding – add about 300 mm (12 in.) to circumference of frame for offcuts
Picture glass, cut to size
Mounting board –heavy artist's board
Backing board – any heavy cardboard
Panel pins (brads) – about 24 per frame
2 screw eyes
Picture hanging wire or string
Brown paper (optional)
Mitre box
Back saw
Hammer
Nail punch
Trimming (utility) knife
Steel ruler
Framing clamp
White glue

Picture framing is getting so expensive that it is worthwhile investing in the few tools you need and learning how to do it yourself. And it is a hobby that can easily be made to pay for itself because your friends will probably start asking you to do their framing as well as soon as they see your results.

It isn't at all difficult to frame a picture adequately, but to do it really well requires a little practice in sawing the mitre and joining the mouldings.

Sawing
If you buy the type of mitre box which has plastic guides at the top, your work will be more accurate. Slide the panel saw through the guides and hold the moulding firmly while you saw.

Measuring the lengths to be cut off can cause problems. The best thing to do is check another frame to see where to mark the moulding. Then, once the mark is lined up with the saw, clamp a small block at the end of the moulding (**4**) to act as a stop. This will guarantee that the opposite moulding is exactly the same length.

The most important point to remember is that the two vertical mouldings *must* be identical in length as must the pair of horizontal mouldings. If they are not, there is no chance that the frame will fit together correctly at the corners. It is advisable to make the frame before you cut the backing boards and order the glass so you can be sure of the exact final size.

When you start framing, buy inexpensive moulding and frame

3 Cut off the end of the moulding in the mitre box. Saw gently using long, smooth strokes.

4 Carefully measure the length of moulding, mark and cut off. Use a clamp to hold it in place.

5 After cutting two pairs of identical sides, glue and clamp tightly using framing clamp.

6 After glue has set, nail panel pins (brads) in corners. Drill small hole first holding frame tightly.

7 Gently set the nails with a nail punch. Then fill the holes with coloured wood filler if desired.

8 Cut out window in mounting or matt board and attach picture to back or glue to front of plain board.

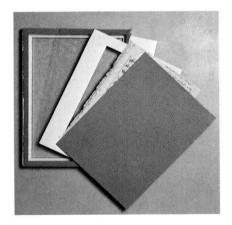

9 The assembly includes the glass, mounting board, picture and backing board. Paper cover is optional.

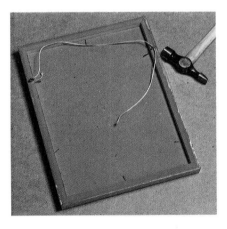

10 Hold assembly in place with pins as shown. Use hook-eyes and wire or string to hang picture.

11 To keep out dust and make a neat job, glue brown wrapping paper to back before adding eyes and string.

12 Glue marbled paper, available from art supply stores, to edges of 6 mm ($\frac{1}{4}$ in.) thick plywood.

13 Assemble the inside and outside frames. Make sure inside frame covers paper completely.

14 Assemble picture, glass etc. in inside frame. Centre it, and screw it to plywood from back.

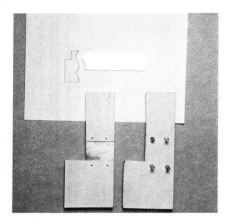

15 Draw moulding shape and make scratch-stock by filing piece of metal and fitting in groove of handle.

16 Use a rabbet plane with fence to cut away rabbet. Make it 10 mm ($\frac{3}{8}$ in.) wide, 6 mm ($\frac{1}{4}$ in.) deep.

17 Scrape back and forth with scraper until the groove is consistent along the length.

pictures which are not too valuable like prints and posters. That way you will gain practice without ruining a masterpiece. After practising on posters and prints you can move on to more detailed and elaborate frames which demand greater skill.

Mouldings

Picture frame mouldings are manufactured in a bewildering variety of shapes, sizes and finishes. You should match the moulding so that it compliments the picture. In other words, a small, delicate picture usually needs a narrow and simple moulding.

Although each style of moulding has a particular name, not many people outside the framing profession remember them. The only terminology that is useful to remember is the 'rabbet' or 'rebate', the little rectangular space along the inside back edge which holds the picture and glass so that the edges don't show.

Most suppliers sell unfinished mouldings which are quite easy to stain or paint yourself. Don't be afraid of painting the frames in bright colours but make sure that they go well with the subject to be framed.

The two 'advanced' examples (**12-14** and **15-20**) show how you can adapt simple, inexpensive materials to make beautiful picture frames. You can even make your own mouldings without any complicated equipment. The only tools required are a rebate plane (**16**) – the replaceable blade type is very useful and a homemade scratch-stock (**15**) which can be filed to shape from an old hacksaw blade or piece of metal.

It is surprisingly easy to experiment with various woods and various shapes of frame.

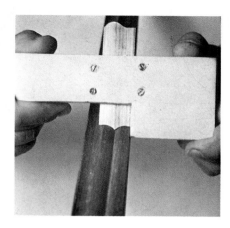

18 Reverse the scraper and mark rest of moulding. Use handle as a guide along the edge.

19 Additional lines can be made with marking gauge. Draw it steadily back and forth.

20 You can use special clips to hold assembly in the frame. To remove simply rotate the clips.

Salt Box

1 Measure for the first side 10 cm (4 in.) long and draw a light, fine line using a carpenter's square.

2 Saw carefully along other side of line, so that the sawn-off piece will measure the actual 10 cm (4 in.)

3 To plane the end, use a block plane with a low angle blade to smooth off the sawn end grain.

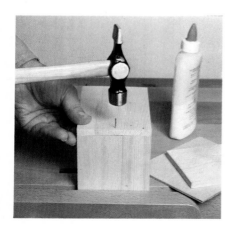

4 After cutting sides and front (see text) put a dab of glue on the ends and nail together.

5 The back can have a decorative shape cut out with a coping saw (see page 35). Nail the back to the sides.

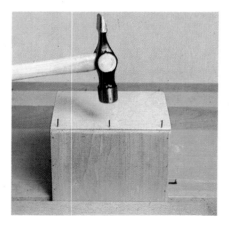

6 Finally measure the base, cut out a piece of plywood to suit and nail and glue it to the bottom.

You will need:
1 piece softwood (pine, spruce)
 100×12 mm (4×½ in.), approx.
 450 mm (18 in.) long
1 piece softwood approx.
 150×12 mm (6×½ in.), approx.
 200 mm (8 in.) long
1 piece plywood 150×120 mm
 (6×5 in.), 4 mm (⅛ in.) thick
24 25-mm (1-in.) panel pins (brads)
Back or hand saw
Hammer
Try square
Block plane (optional)
Ruler or tape measure
Pencil

Many people insist that they cannot saw along a straight line. Don't be so pessimistic. If you use a sharp saw and hold the wood securely sawing is much easier. Practise by cutting off a small board three or four times. It is almost guaranteed that by the fourth time your sawcut will be straight and accurate.

Sawing
A power table saw is fast and accurate and there is no way hand cutting can compete with it. But many people prefer to saw by hand.

The important thing to remember about sawing is to keep the saw sharp. You can sharpen a saw yourself (see pages 62-63).

Saws
Saws are available in many shapes and sizes but, basically, they all do either one of two jobs: ripping or cross-cutting. Ripping is sawing along the grain, and cross-cutting means cutting across the grain.

The difference between a rip saw and a cross-cut saw is the number, and hence the size, of teeth per inch of saw. Rip saws have 5-6 points or teeth per inch whereas cross-cuts saws have between 8 and 32 points.

Saws are divided into categories according to their use. A general purpose saw (8 points) is most useful for the beginner; it will cross-cut well and also rip in small quantities. A back saw is usually about 250-300 mm (10-12 in.) long with a stiffened blade to allow straight, accurate cuts. It is a useful general purpose saw for all but heavy work. There are also specialist's saws such as dovetail saws (16 points) and bead saws (16-20 points). (See pages 8-9.)

Measuring the wood
Remember that a wood size, say 1.2×10 cm (½×4 in.) is a nominal size. That is, these were the dimensions when the wood was sawn in the mill. After sawing, the wood is passed through a planer which shaves off a thin layer of wood and leaves a smooth surface. The 1.2×10 cm (½×4 in.) planed section (as you buy it) will therefore measure about 0.9×9.5cm (⅜×3¾ in.). So in planning the box keep in mind that you should use the actual and not the nominal dimensions.

Making the salt box
All boxes have four sides and a bottom. Some have a top, which can be either the lift-off, the hinged, or the sliding type. Draw the salt box on paper.

The salt box has the simplest joints of all: one piece of wood is butted up against the next and simply nailed to hold it in place (the glue is added for a little extra strength). First measure and cut the two side pieces out of the 12×100 mm (½×4 in.) softwood. Make them 100 mm (4 in.) long (**2**). If you have a block plane (**3**) you can then smooth the sawn ends carefully.

Then cut the front piece exactly the same width as the wood for the back (12×150 mm (½×6 in.)). Once the back is cut 190 mm (7½ in.) long and the heart shape has been cut out with a coping saw, the four sides can be nailed together (see **6, 7, 8** page 35).

Measure the overall size of the bottom and cut off a piece of plywood to fit. You will probably find that the corners don't fit exactly right. Try to sand them so that they look smooth and even, but if the fit is bad, fill the gaps with wood filler and paint the box after sanding smooth (see pages 60-61).

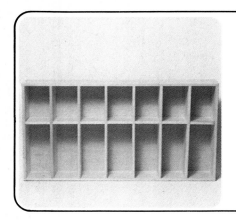

Storage Rack

You will need:
Softwood (pine or similar)
  100× 12 mm (4× ½ in.), approx
  5 m (16 ft) long
1 piece plywood approx.
  600× 300 mm (24× 12 in.),
  4 mm (⅛ in.) thick
About 48 25-mm (1-in.) panel
  pins (brads)
Hand saw or back saw
Chisel 6 mm (¼ in.) wide
Hammer
Mallet
Nail punch
Sandpaper
White glue

All kitchens need storage space for jars, cans, spices and cannisters and, rather than hiding all these away behind cupboard doors, why not display them in open storage racks like this? You can adapt this technique when building larger storage units for cans or dishes and make them become part of the decoration of a kitchen. Or you could use this kind of rack for storing jars of spices. This sort of storage unit should also be handy over a desk or any other working surface for storing paperwork or nails and screws.

Planning the work
Planning the work out carefully on

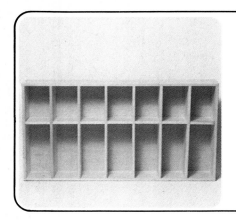

1 With a sharp pencil mark a line lightly against a piece of the wood. Mark it exactly half the width.

2 After sawing inside the two lines remove the waste wood with a chisel and mallet. Tap it at an angle.

3 Clean off the cut so that it is square and exactly to the mark. Then try to slot in another piece.

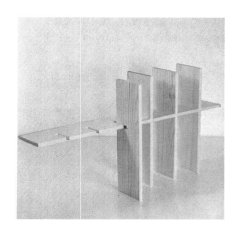

4 Make six slots in the horizontal piece and position the six verticals, using a mallet if necessary.

paper is always important, particularly here where the there are so many pieces and such precise dimensions.

Draw the cabinet, indicating on the drawing the length of each piece. Also make a drawing of each component giving such details as where the slots are to be cut. This way, when it comes to doing the sawing, you'll be much less likely to make mistakes and to forget how the rack is put together.

Cutting the pieces

There are eight short pieces all 300 mm (12 in.) long. Six of these have a slot across exactly half the width. The other two pieces are left uncut. Of the three long horizontal pieces which are 60 cm (24 in.) long, only one has slots; the other two are used for the surround, top and bottom, and do not need to be cut.

Making the slots

The pieces fit like the divisions in a cardboard bottle-box. It is important that they fit snugly so make sure that you measure carefully first using a piece of wood (1) and then saw carefully inside the lines so that the opening

is the same width as the wood.

Saw on the inside of each line and stop at the mark indicating the half width.

Then use a chisel and mallet to remove the wood, making first an angled and then a vertical cut. Remember to protect the work surface underneath from the chisel.

Slant the first stroke slightly (2) and the wood should break away easily. Then, to square off the hole, slide down vertically without the mallet (3). The slot should be about 170 mm (7 in.) up from the bottom on each of the six vertical

pieces. For the horizontal piece, divide the length into seven equal compartments, keeping in mind the thickness of the verticals. It doesn't really matter if the compartments aren't exactly the same. In fact, it may look more interesting if you vary them, or if you add another horizontal shelf.

Finishing

It will probably look best to let the storage rack stay a natural pine so after sanding thoroughly simply give it one or two coats of clear polyurethane varnish (see pages 60-61).

5 Nail on the two short ends, nail the long surrounds to each vertical. Check that pieces are straight.

6 Drive the nails below the surface with a nail punch. You can then fill the holes with wood stopper.

7 Measure the overall size and cut the plywood backing to fit. Glue and nail down.

Dish Rack

You will need:
2 pieces of softwood (pine)
    50 × 25 mm (2 × 1 in.), 500 mm
    (20 in.) long
12 or 15 mm ($\frac{1}{2}$ or $\frac{5}{8}$ in.)
    diameter dowelling, approx.
    3 m (10 ft) long
Back saw or hand saw
Brace with drill bit to match
    diameter of dowels
Try square (optional)
Ruler or tape measure
White glue

One of the difficulties with wood is that it is usually cumbersome to join two pieces together securely.

The basic problem is that pieces of wood are rectangular and making rectangular slots or notches to fit them together requires considerable skill. So, traditionally, most of the joiner's time and energy was taken up by devising and perfecting ways to fit wood together tightly and securely. And these are still the best ways to join wood. (See also pages 53-55.)

It is much easier to make a round than a square hole. All you do is use the drill with the proper diameter drill bit and drill it to the required depth.

This is precisely why working with dowels is so useful. It makes joinery very much easier.

Instead of all the chiseling and sawing to make the rectangular fittings in, say, a mortise and tenon joint, you simply drill matching holes in two pieces of wood and glue short lengths of dowel to both. There are, of course, many instances where the traditional joints are preferable, but dowelled joints are an important time-saver especially for the home carpenter without much equipment.

Dowels
Dowels are usually made from

1 Mark the holes with a nail or centre punch before drilling to keep the drill bit from slipping.

2 Set out the holes at 62 mm (2½ in.) centres. Use a carpenter's square as a check to keep brace vertical.

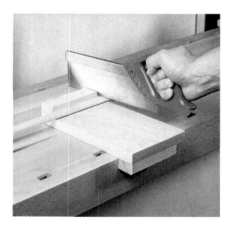

3 Cut off 150 mm (6 in.) lengths of dowel using a bench hook, made from plywood and two wood strips.

hardwood such as birch or ramin, although the larger diameters – above 25 mm (1 in.) – are soft-wood.

Dowels are made by pulling a piece of square wood through a series of round holes each one smaller than the last until the desired diameter is reached.

Using the drill

The smaller drill is called a hand drill (see page 6). It uses drill bits up to 6 mm ($\frac{1}{4}$ in.) in diameter. The brace, however, drills holes from about 6 mm ($\frac{1}{4}$ in.) to about 38 mm ($1\frac{1}{2}$ in.) with normal auger drill bits and to about 75 mm (3 in.) diameter with special, ex-pandable drill bits. The brace is what you will need for this project.

To fit the bit in the drill, simply turn the chuck, the part that holds the bit, until the opening is wide enough. Then push in the drill bit and tighten by holding the chuck while turning the handle.

Start every hole by first making an indentation with a nail or a special centre punch. This keeps the drill bit from slipping away from the centre.

When drilling, remember to hold the brace vertically. Check by standing a carpenter's square nearby (**2**). If the hole is to stop part of the way through, use either a home-made 'gauge' (see **4**, page 16-17) or stop and check the depth intermittently.

Dish rack

This dish rack couldn't be simpler to make. After cutting the two lengths of 25×50 mm (1×2 in.) wood, cut holes at 62 mm ($2\frac{1}{2}$ in.) intervals starting 30 mm ($1\frac{1}{4}$ in.) in from the end.

Drill the holes all the way through remembering to protect the work surface. After drilling eight holes through each piece, drill two more holes part-way through each edge for the two

4 The two drilled supports attached with dowels at either end. They are about 90 mm ($3\frac{1}{2}$ in.) apart.

5 Glue the dowel pieces in place. Adjust them before the glue sets to make them perfectly straight.

connecting dowels (**4**).

Then cut the dowels to length, 150 mm (6 in.). A bench hook (**3**) is most useful for cutting off short lengths of wood. You can make it from a piece of plywood approximately 150×250 mm (6× 10 in.) and two pieces of straight softwood glued and screwed to opposite ends as shown.

Before you glue the dowels in place, round the exposed end with sandpaper. Then with all the dowels in position, give the whole dish rack two coats of clear polyurethane varnish. You can use the same method to make similar racks for coats and hats, towels and toast.

Plant rack

The plant rack shown here looks a little more complicated but only because of the added plywood frills. The basic structure is quite simple: four 50×50 mm (2×2 in.) uprights with holes at 100 mm (4 in.) centres staggered 50 mm (2 in.) in each direction. The dowels are then pushed through and used as a support either for a shelf for standing plants, or for hanging plants on the dowel pegs themselves.

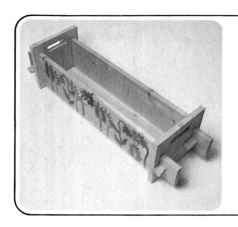

Window Box

1 If the wood is too wide, you can saw it to the required width with a rip saw.

2 After sawing, smooth to exact dimensions using plane. The jack plane is used for long joints.

3 Draw a line 100 mm (4 in.) from each end. Use a marking gauge to mark 35 mm ($1\frac{3}{8}$ in.) from each edge.

4 Parallel lines show thickness of end piece. Note the hole marked out for peg in centre.

You will need:
2 pieces softwood for sides
    200 × 25 mm (8 × 1 in.), 900 mm
    (3 ft) long
2 pieces softwood for ends
    250 × 25 mm (10 × 1 in.),
    250 mm (10 in.) long
1 piece plywood 700 × 160mm
    (28 × $6\frac{1}{2}$ in.), 9 or 12 mm ($\frac{3}{8}$ or
    $\frac{1}{2}$ in.) thick
Rip saw (optional)
Chisel, 12 or 19 mm ($\frac{1}{2}$ or $\frac{3}{4}$ in.)
wide
Brace with auger drill bits
Marking gauge
Mallet
Plane (optional)

Here is a new design for a window box. It has handles for easy carrying and legs so that the bottom is off the ground. It comes apart for easy storage and it is assembled without nails or screws.

Making the window box will demonstrate several very useful principles in joinery. Most of the traditional joints (see pages 53-55) use a rectangular slot through which the wood is fastened. This window box has four passing tenons – a term for slotting one piece of wood through another and holding it securely with a peg.

Ripping and planing wood
Although it probably won't be

necessary to cut down the width of a board for this window box it is a useful technique to know and it will no doubt come in handy.

First draw the guide line and then using a rip saw (5-6 teeth to the inch, see page 6) cut about 2 mm $\frac{1}{16}$ in.) outside the line (1). To smooth down the wood to the exact dimension desired, use a jack plane or a smoothing plane.

Planes

Like most other woodworking tools, planes are available in many shapes and sizes, each with a particular purpose.

The jointer plane is the long 'work horse' plane between 450 and 560 mm (18 and 22 in.) long. It is used for general levelling and for planing square edges. The jack plane which is 350-380 mm (14-15 in.) long is also a general purpose plane.

The smoothing plane, about 250 mm (10 in.) long, is probably the easiest for a beginner to handle so it should be the first plane you buy.

The block plane, 150-180 mm (6-7 in.) long is for small work. One type of block plane has its blade at a low angle (12°) so that it can be used to clean up across the end grain (see 3, page 44).

Besides these general use planes the rabbet plane is quite handy. It has a fence to keep it parallel to the work and is used to cut a rabbet or a step into the piece (see 16 page 42). The combination plane (8) can be used with a variety of cutting blades to cut grooves, rabbets and brads.

Cutting the holes

If, when marking the lines for the holes, you use a marking or cutting gauge (3, 4) you'll find that it forms an accurate starting groove for the chisels. And before using the chisel, try to remove as much

5   Remove each side with two saw cuts. After drilling, use chisel to make rectangular peg hole.

7   To hold in bottom, nail and glue strips along the bottom edge. The bottom fits between the sides.

9   The end piece has a handle and two slots to receive the sides. Drill before using a chisel.

6   The bull nose plane is useful for smoothing off areas which are awkward and hard to reach.

8   Alternatively, you can make a groove with a special combination plane with interchangeable blades.

10   Make five or six holes in bottom. Tap in pegs with mallet until the joint is tight.

wood as possible by first drilling safely between the lines.

Mark both sides so that you can turn the work over to drill and chisel from both sides. Otherwise the wood may split underneath.

Finishing the window box
You can add your own personal touch by cutting one or two stencils out of cardboard and spray painting flowers or leaves through them. Be careful to mask the surrounding area when you spray paint. Finish with three coats of polyurethane varnish or paint.

11 Decorate the window box by stencilling flowers and leaves on the sides with spray paint.

WOODWORKING JOINTS
Today most wood is sawn, planed, cut up and put together by machines. There is a machine for almost every technique imaginable. Although there is certainly nothing wrong with machines, they tend to take the craft and satisfaction out of woodworking.

Here you will find an introduction to a few of the better known joinery methods. Anyone who wants to learn more should refer to some of the excellent books available on furniture making and joinery.

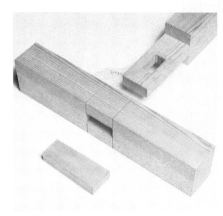

1 The components of a tongue-in-groove joint. Cut the grooves with a table saw.

2 Cut the tongue so that it fits into the grooves easily and leaves room at the sides for excess glue.

3 A loose tenon joint. The tenon (hole) is usually just over a third of the thickness. Notice wedged peg.

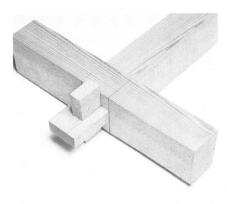

4 The fixing is strong and secure without glue or screws. It can be taken apart in seconds.

Traditional furniture making

New plastic furniture can be moulded in one piece but wood has to be joined in sections.

A table is a typical example. Because boards come in certain widths, several have to be joined side by side to make an area wide enough for the top. Since wood shrinks and warps as it dries, it has to be dried slowly after it is sawed into boards: it is stacked in the open air for 12 months. Today most of this drying is done in kilns.

The boards are then planed so that the sides are straight and true. Then matching grooves are cut into the edges of the planks and a thin sliver of wood, the tongue (**1** and **2**), is put between the boards as they are glued together. Each board is arranged with its annual rings opposite the next so that they don't warp the same way. Then the top surface is planed again, diagonally at first, until it is straight and true.

Now consider the base of the table. The top usually has to be supported along all four edges and in the middle. Each rail or support then has to be made to receive the top either by pegging, screwing or notching.

The rails cannot just be screwed to the legs; that isn't good joinery. Instead, a hole or mortise is cut in the top of two faces of each leg. Then a matching tenon is shaped out of the end of each rail (**9** and **10**) so that when pushed into the mortise, the fit will be so tight that the table will be rigid and secure, with little or no glue.

A really good joiner will design the joints so that, should the wood expand or contract, it won't show in the joint.

Tools

You can do most joinery with a fairly limited selection of tools, but there comes a point when 'special' tools are necessary. Whether or not you can justify the expense depends entirely on how much work you plan to do with them. If you are only going to need them once or twice, find a substitute.

In addition to the basic tool kit, the following tools will be useful for joinery work: a good 300 mm (12 in.) panel saw for general use. A dovetail saw, 200 mm (8 in.) long with 18-22 points for making dovetails and also for all fine work. A saw set and file to sharpen saws (see pages 62-63).

As well as the basic set of bevelled edge chisels of 6, 12, 19 mm ($\frac{1}{4}$, $\frac{1}{2}$, $\frac{3}{4}$ in.) you will need a 3 mm ($\frac{1}{8}$ in.) chisel and also a 12 mm ($\frac{1}{2}$ in.) mortise chisel.

A basic tool kit may or may not include the 220 mm (9 in.) smoothing plane for general work. If it doesn't, this plane should be added for joinery work. You will also need a 350 mm (14 in.) jack plane and the smaller 150 mm (6 in.) block plane. Eventually a rabbet plane with fence is useful. There is a new type available with replaceable blades. Other planes which have more specialist functions are the router plane, combination plane and moulding

5 Dovetailed joints are very strong. Cut the tail on the right first and use it to make the pins.

6 A dovetail joint, whether lapped, secret or carted, is glued and tapped together with a mallet.

7 A halved joint. When the timbers are equal, remove half the depth from each.

8 Here the bolt heads become a feature of the joint. Otherwise, hide screws and bolts with dowel pegs.

plane.

Other useful joinery tools include cabinet scrapers, marking gauges, G-cramps (C-clamps) and, of course, a few electric hand tools such as a jig saw (sabre saw).

Planning the work

Before you start plan out the project carefully, drawing it, and any difficult components to scale if possible and prepare a cutting list, giving all the various pieces. Then buy the wood and store it carefully to allow the timber to adjust to its new moisture conditions. If the wood has been well dried, you can begin immediately. Otherwise, leave it for a few weeks and, if it warps, plane it straight.

Before you begin the detailed work of preparing joints, rabbets etc., saw all the pieces to length, squaring the ends and checking for any defects in the wood.

Basic joinery technique

For a relative beginner, the large variety of woodworking joints may, at first, seem very confusing. But you will find that, just as you gradually acquire more tools as you learn more techniques, you will also build up a repertoire of woodworking joints.

Woodworking joints can be divided into three rough categories: butted joints, interlocking joints and mechanical joints.

There are first of all, the various kinds of joints where boards are butted up to one another, either end to end or side to side.

The salt box (page 44) and the spice rack (page 46) involve the use of very simple butt joints. In the salt box two pieces are joined at the corner by nailing and gluing. For the storage rack, the vertical dividers and the middle shelf are all simply butted up against the surrounding pieces and nailed.

A nailed joint is usually unsatisfactory in joinery, but spice jars are so light that nailed joints are adequate. You can, of course, make a groove, or housed joint, on the inside of the surround pieces to strengthen it.

Butted joints include joining boards edge to edge, as for example for a table top. The edges can be simply glued together, or, if the loads are heavy, strengthened with a tongue (**1** and **2**) or with dowel pegs inserted into matching boards.

For most connections not involving metal fasteners, the two members are interlocked by removing a portion of each piece; these are called interlocking joints. A dovetail joint (**5** and **6**) which is quite demanding to make, is still one of the strongest joints in woodworking.

Dovetail joints are used in the making of all good drawers to connect the front to the sides so that they stay solidly joined.

A much simpler joint is the halved joint (**7** and **8**) which is used for the storage rack. Halved joints are most frequently used for making up frame works such as for inexpensive door frames and for some furniture. They can be held in place either with screws or bolts.

Mortise and tenon joints (**9** and **10**) are probably the most familiar of all woodworking joints. They are used in most furniture, particularly in tables, desks etc. where the rails are connected to the legs. There are many variations of mortise and tenons. Pictures **9** and **10** show a fairly complicated version called a secret haunched tenon. In other types the tenon passes directly through the wood. It can either stop flush and be wedged tightly in place (a wedged through mortise and tenon) or it can be fixed with a peg (**3** and **4**) – a loose tenon. This joint is frequently used in making refectory tables.

In some applications you will find a mechanical joint is simplest.

Mechanical joints include the familiar screwed and bolted joints which are particularly useful for quick, strong joints. But they require careful installation in order to hide all the screws. The members should either be attached from underneath or behind or the screw heads can be hidden with dowel pegs planed flush with the surface.

Today there are so many ingenious mechanical fasteners on the market that they are too numerous to mention. They include several devices which allow the furniture to be knocked down quickly for moving or storing. The best way to find out about mechanical fixings is to look around and ask questions at a large hardware store.

The kitchen table shown here uses several examples of woodworking joints. The top is tongue-in-groove boards. The sides are screwed in place with the screws hidden with dowel pegs. The base structure has loose tenons and is fixed to the legs with a bolted halved joint.

9 A mortise-in-tenon joint. This example shows the secret haunch which strengthens the joint.

10 The joint leaves no trace of a fixing and is best left flush on the face and top.

Turned Candlesticks

1 A selection of turning tools

2 The lathe can be a single unit like this one or a less expensive, bench-mounted model.

You will need:
2 pieces hardwood approx.
  50 × 50 mm (2 × 2 in.) 100 mm
  (4 in.) long
Lathe
Set of turning tools: 2 or 3
  gouges, 1 flat scraper, rounded
  scraper, 2 or 3 chisels and a
  parting tool
Brace with 19 mm ($\frac{3}{4}$ in.) auger
  bit
G-cramps (C-clamps)
Ruler

Of all the different types of woodworking, turning gives the most satisfaction. Even to the most experienced craftsman there is a touch of magic in the way that a square, rough piece of wood is transformed into a delicate object in moments. Not everyone will be able to buy a lathe but simple bench-mounted lathes can be bought quite inexpensively and bolted down solidly to a home-made bench top.

Turning can be quite dangerous if it is done carelessly or with dull tools which bite into the wood and tear off large chunks which then fly off.

Follow the manufacturer's instructions for sharpening carefully. There is no need for the

3 Find the centre by crossing the ends. Then use a nail or centre punch to mark the centre point.

4 Mount the wood between the four-pronged centre on the left and the tail centre on the right.

5 To rough down length of wood, slant gouge slightly upwards and rest it and your hand on the tool rest.

6 After piece is round, use the scraper to smooth down surface. Remember to keep tools sharp.

7 Check diameter against drawing, using either calipers or a home-made cardboard template.

frequent sharpening required in carving, but having a grinding wheel on which to sharpen turning tools would prove very handy.

In the first candlestick project the work is turned between the centres of the lathe. This is quite safe and easy. There is no need to plane off the edges of the square wood first. You can rough down any piece of wood into a smooth cylinder on the lathe using a gouge in a matter of minutes.

Using a gouge
The gouge is the workhorse of the lathe tools. It is used to rough down all work and even to get some types of work smooth enough to sand. Before it is used the gouge should be ground on the wheel so that its end goes straight across.

When removing waste wood with a gouge, start at one end and traverse the length of the wood back and forth. As you move the gouge sideways, hold it firmly with your right hand against the body for support, and rest it on the tool rest with the left hand gently guiding it on the rest.

As you guide the tool along the wood, the gouge should be rolled slightly toward the direction of travel, so that the entire cutting surface is used. But beware of the back, or trailing edge. It tends to bite into the wood and tear it.

Be extra careful turning the outside of a bowl because the gouge tends to dig into the end grain. The solution is to hold the gouge at a steep angle so that the ground surface rubs on the wood and the edge cuts into the wood instead of scraping it. Then, if the tool is sharp and held firmly, the work should go smoothly.

Turning the inside of a bowl is not quite as difficult. Start at

8 Use a V-tool to cut off a piece entirely, or to add delicate detail to the work.

9 Add detail like this rounded groove by using a small gouge or rounded scraper.

10 After the piece is sanded on the lathe, drill the candle hole with a brace.

11 Glue the two halves with matching grooves together before turning. The surfaces must be perfectly flat.

12 After turning, drill hole through side at base and a larger shallow hole in bottom to pass cord through.

the edge and gradually work towards the centre taking off a thin layer with each passing of the gouge. With the laminated bowl (**14-20**) the glued joints tend to catch in the turning tools so the thinner you make the glued surface the better.

Scrapers and chisels

The finer work is done with scrapers and chisels. Scrapers are ground to a flat face similar to a cabinet scraper, and are used to finish off turning pieces. Chisels have both sides ground to a tapered edge and cut into the wood like a chisel as it turns. Chisels must be kept sharp to be effective so it is therefore wiser to limit their use to finer work. The trailing edge of the chisel also tends to bite into the work, so the cutting should be done with all but the last section of the chisel edge.

Sanding

Sanding is very straightforward. Just remove the tool rest and apply sandpaper (folded three or four times) against the rotating wood. Don't try to sand away faults that should be removed with a chisel or scraper. With very porous woods like mahogany it is

13 Push brass fitting into enlarged hole at top and thread on the lamp holder.

advisable to add a sanding sealer (see pages 60-61) before you apply a finish to the sanded wood.

Finishing

You can apply any finish to turned work that you would use on other wood surfaces, and most finishes can be applied to the sanded wood as it revolves on the lathe.

LAMP
You will need:
2 pieces hardwood approx.
  75 × 38 mm (3 × 1½ in.), 200 mm (8 in.) long
Electrical cord
Lamp holder with threaded sleeve
Lampshade
White glue
Tools: as for candlesticks

BOWL
You will need:
1 piece hardwood (teak or similar) for sides approx. 50 × 30 mm (2 × 1¼ in.), 900 mm (3 ft) long
1 piece hardwood for base approx. 250 × 12 mm (10 × ½ in.), 250 mm (10 in.) long, or 2 pieces 125 mm (5 in.) wide joined together
Plywood for template 300 × 300 mm (12 × 12 in.), any thickness
Tools: as for candlesticks
Back saw
Plane
Compass and protractor
String

If the bowl is to be used as a salad bowl, it is best to give it three coats of clear matt polyurethane, rubbing between coats with wire wool. But for most work, wax polishing is the best method of finishing. You can use any wax polish intended for wood but beeswax, if you can get it, it gives a deep and lustrous shine (see pages 60-61).

14 Make a careful template of pieces. Divide circle into nine 40° segments and draw pieces.

15 Cut pieces a little larger than final size. Make a template with 70° angle to mark each cutting line.

16 Make a shooting board with plywood base and guide set at 70° angle. Plane both ends to exact dimension.

17 Glue the nine pieces together and hold tight with cord. Then glue and clamp to base.

18 Screw plywood to back and mounting plate to plywood. This must be centred on back.

19 Roughen outside with a sharp gouge held low against body. Be careful not to dig in back edge of gouge.

20 Work the inside from edge toward centre, first with gouge and later with scraper.

Finishing

1 Apply polyurethane varnish with a brush along the grain. Thin the first coat.

2 When varnish is thoroughly dry, rub down with steel wire wool to remove all imperfections.

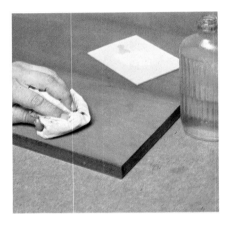

3 After three or four coats, rub down with a rag moistened in linseed oil and dipped in pumice powder.

Today with the availability of modern proprietary polishes and varnishes, much of the tedious work has been taken out of polishing. But no matter which method you use, the more work you do in sanding and rubbing down, and the more coats you apply, the more luxurious the finish to the wood.

There are several ways of finishing wood. You can, of course, leave the wood totally untreated; just sanded smooth as is done with scrubbed pine kitchen tables. But most wood needs some protection.

You can protect wood by using oil, wax, shellac, varnish, lacquer or any combination of these.

Sanding

All but carved wood needs to be sanded. Sandpaper, glasspaper or garnet paper all have small, hard granules glued to a backing paper to produce an abrasive surface and are available in a variety of grades.

Always sand along the grain. Sanding across the grain leaves scratches which show up even more when the finish is added. Start with rough or medium sand-

paper and use a cork or wooden block as a backing. As the wood gets smoother, progress to a finer paper working down to the very finest garnet papers. The grade of the final paper used will determine the final smoothness.

Some woods such as oak or mahogany, which have coarse grains are are very porous, tend to polish unevenly so use wood filler to seal the pores. (Not wood stopper which is used to fill cracks and holes.)

Stain and bleach

To lighten the colour of any wood,

you can apply one of two types of bleach. Chlorinated laundry bleach is the weakest, and therefore the safest to use. Oxalic acid which can be weakened with a cool solution of borax is much stronger.

To apply bleach, use synthetic brushes and wear rubber gloves at all times. Remember bleaches are dangerous and if any gets on your skin, particularly any oxalic acid, wash it off immediately.

There are many types of water, alcohol or oil based stain available. Before you stain wood, make sure that the surface is clean and entirely free from any stain, wax or old finish. It is best to follow the manufacturer's instructions and to use it on a small area first to test the intensity of the colour.

Adding liquid to bare wood raises the grain and makes the surface rough, so before applying stain or bleach, wipe the surface with a damp cloth. Then when it has dried, sand it off with fine paper.

Oiling

Oil is usually applied on top of a sealing coat but in some instances it can be used directly on the bare wood. Teak oil, for example, is used directly on the surface of teak (**4**). Oil finishes are not as durable as the other finishes and the surface will require intermittant re-oiling.

The most popular formula is linseed oil warmed with equal parts of pure turpentine. Rub the mixture into the wood with a soft cloth and allow it to soak in before any excess is removed. Repeat this procedure several times.

Waxing

Wax is applied directly on the wood or, more often, on top of a sealer layer. You can use pro-prietary waxes, but beeswax or carnauba wax give a more lustrous finish.

Heat the beeswax or carnauba wax with enough turpentine to make it the consistency of paste. The wax can be a mixture of four parts beeswax to one part carnauba wax. Apply liberally to the wood surface, allow to dry and then polish and buff hard to get a good polish.

Varnishing

The traditional shellac French polishing method has been largely replaced by the modern synthetic varnishes. These varnishes are extremely tough and durable.

The easiest finish for the home craftsman to apply is polyurethane varnish. It is available in clear (either matt or gloss) finish and in a variety of colours. After the wood has been sanded, brush on the varnish (**1**). Allow the first coat to dry well and then rub down with fine steel wire wool available from hardware stores (**2**). Build up three or four layers like this rubbing with steel wire wool after each coat is dry.

After the final coat, rub down the varnish with a rag moistened with linseed oil and dipped in pumice powder to get a deep polish (**3**).

Painting

First fill all cracks and holes with wood stopper (**5**) and sand the surface smooth. Then apply the first base coat. After this coat is dry, sand lightly with fine paper and add one or two more coats depending on the paint and the finish required.

4 Some woods like teak can be protected with an application of oil. Rub in several coats before buffing.

5 Before painting wood, fill all cracks and holes with plain or matching wood stopper.

6 Paint the wood with two or three coats sanding lightly with fine sandpaper between each coat.

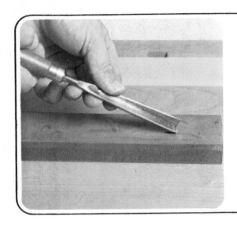

Sharpening

1 If the chisel, plane iron or gouge gets very full or nicked, grind it on a grinding wheel.

2 For frequent sharpening, rub chisel on oiled stone giving it an even, shiny bevel across edge.

3 Remove burr by rubbing back and forth across oil stone. Feel the edge for sharpness.

In many ways sharpening is the most important part of wood-working. No one can get good results with dull tools.

Buy a good oil stone (**2, 3, 4**) and make a special wooden box for it with a lift-off cover and a couple of fine pins which protrude from the bottom of the box enough to grip the work bench when you are using the stone.

You will also need a slip stone (**5**) which is a small stone used to remove the burr after the correct bevel has been achieved on the oil stone. (**3**). The best type of slip stone is Arkansas stone.

Chisels are bevel ground at the factory but before you use them you must give the tip a slightly steeper bevel. Rub back and forth on the stone (moistened with a little oil) until the chisel has an even bevel. This rubbing forces the metal at the tip to curl back over the top. This is called the burr. To finish the edge properly rub the back side along the stone several times (**3**).

Be careful not to wear a groove in the centre of the stone by always rubbing in the same place. Move the chisel from side to side on the stone while sharpening.

Sharpen plane irons in precisely the same way. You can use a special device (**4**) which keeps it at the recommended angle.

Give your gouges a bevel by rubbing them back and forth across the stone. To keep the gouge from side to side as well as pushing it back and forth. Since you can't remove the burr with a flat stone, use a small, hand-held slip stone (**5**) and rub it back and forth along the inside of the curve.

Carving tools, in addition to being sharpened on a stone, must be stropped with a piece of leather glued to a wood strip (**6**).

4 Sharpen plane iron the same way. Optional holding device keeps it at the correct angle.

For very blunt or nicked tools you will need a grinding wheel to achieve a sharp surface. Once the correct bevel is on the tool, it can be sharpened on an oil stone.

Saws

It is not advisable for the beginner to sharpen saws. Most hardware stores know a 'saw doctor' who will do it. Basically the procedure is to set the teeth at the correct angle with a saw set (**7**). Once the teeth are set, they are then filed – cross cut saws at 45° (**8**) and rip saws straight across at 90° (**9**).

Drill bits

Drill bits rarely need sharpening. Use a special small file first to sharpen the two vertical cutting edges along the inside sides (**10**). Then use the file to sharpen the two horizontal cutting edges.

5 Remove burr on inside of curve by rubbing with hand-held slip stone. A flat stone cannot be used for this.

6 Final 'razor edge' is achieved by stropping on a piece of leather glued to wood.

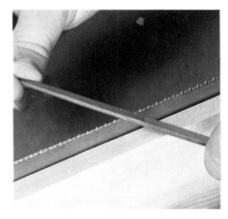

7 A saw-set is used to adjust teeth. Each type of saw has teeth set to a different angle.

8 A triangular file is used to sharpen the teeth. For cross-cut saws it is held at a 45° angle.

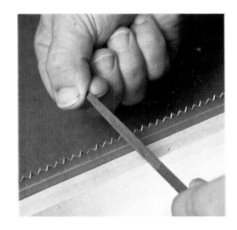

9 File rip saws at 90°. Alternative teeth are sharpened from opposite directions.

10 To sharpen auger drill bit, first file inside of the vertical cutting edges.

List of suppliers

Some further reading

The Art and Practice of Marquetry, W. A. Lincoln, Thames and Hudson, London, 1971; Scribner, New York, 1974

Game Bird Carving, Bruce Burk, Winchester Press, New York, 1972

Picture Framing for Beginners, Prudence Nuttall, Studio Vista, London, 1968

Practical Veneering, Charles Hayward, Evans, London, 1961

Practical Woodturner, F. Pain, Evans, London, 1957; Drake, New York, 1970

The Technique of Furniture Making, Ernest Joyce, Batsford, London, 1970

What Wood is That? A Manual of Wood Identification, Herbert Edlin, Thames and Hudson, London, 1969; Viking Press, New York, 1969

Wood Carving, Techniques and Projects, James Johnstone, Sunset, Lane Books, California, 1971

Wood Finishing, John Collier, Pergamon Press, Oxford, and New York, 1967

Woodwork Joints, Charles Hayward, Evans, London, 1949; Drake, New York, 1970

The Woodworker's Pocket Book, Charles Hayward, Evans, London, 1971

Woodworking Tools, Frederick Oughton, Constable, London, 1973

DATE DUE